ISBN 978-0-483-17312-5
PIBN 10444496

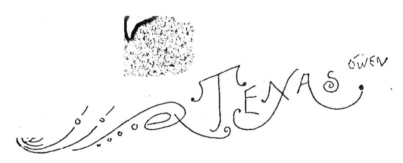

COMPLETE GUID TO TEXAS

OWEN

PUBLISHED BY

DEALY & BAKER,

STATIONERS AND PRINTERS,

HOUSTON, TEXAS.

Price, 10 Cents.

VISIT HOUSTON'S MODERN SUBURB, **HOUSTON HEIGHTS**

HOUSTON HEIGHTS BOULEVARD.

Houston Heights

ELECTRIC LIGHT AND WATER WORKS PLANTS.

531

Omaha an

504 Travis

Copyrigh

No. 2. APRIL, 1895.

COMPLETE

GUIDE TO HOUSTON,

TEXAS.

PLACES IN HOUSTON

...AND...

HOW TO FIND THEM.

PUBLISHED BY
DEALY & BAKER,
STATIONERS, PRINTERS AND BLANK BOOK MAKERS,
No. 211 FANNIN ST., HOUSTON, TEX.

ALPHABETICAL INDEX.

INDEX TO ADVERTISEMENTS.

STREETS AND NUMBERS.

Broadly speaking, the principal streets in Houston run north and south, east and west.

Main street, in the center of the city, runs south from the bayou.

All streets running parallel with Main are designated as "streets;" all running at right angles to Main are called "avenues."

One hundred numbers are allowed to a block, so that one can tell from the number the distance from a designated place.

Main street is numbered from the bayou south, so that No. 601 is the seventh block from the bayou.

The city is divided into districts, with a named street as a base, the numbers on the avenues or cross streets run east and west from the base line, dividing at 1000. Example: Main Street District, Congress Avenue, No. 900 is in first block west, and No. 1001 is in first block east; No. 501 is in the fifth block west, and No. 1501 is in sixth block east.

The actual points of the compass as relates to Main street are thus:

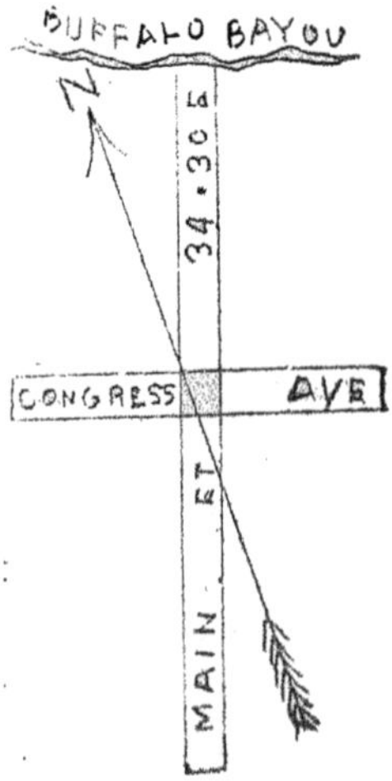

HOUSTON.

SHORTLY after the battle of San Jacinto, April 21, 1836, A. C. & J. K. Allen, located the City of Houston.

On May 5, 1836, the Congress of the Republic met in adjourned session, and from that date until 1840, Houston was the Capital of the Republic. For a short time after that date—in 1842–1844, it was again the Capital City.

In locating at the head of tide-water on Buffalo Bayou, our fathers builded better than they knew, for the location has given our city a commercial advantage not shared by any other city in the State. The bayou, with its direct "deep-water" connection, gives the city the benefit of "water competitive rates." This, with the twelve railroads centering here, makes Houston the best distributing point in Texas.

"All Railroads in Texas lead to Houston."

Secretary Hester, of the New Orleans Cotton Exchange, in his last report gives the cotton "deliveries" for six months ending February 28th, at 8,467,655 bales, of which Texas furnished 2,893,396 bales, or over 34 per cent. of the whole.

At the same date, Secretary Kidd, of the Houston Cotton Exchange, reported that the gross receipts of Houston, had reached 1,629,023 bales—56.3 per cent. of the Texas crop, or 19.2 per cent. of the whole deliveries.

These receipts stand second only to those of New

Orleans, and show Houston to be the largest interior cotton receiving port in the United States.

The value of our bayou to Houston, and the State at large, is best seen when we note that of cotton only, there were shipped from September 30th to March 8th, via the bayou, 455,254 bales, of which 182,000 were delivered at ship's side in the stream, saving all drayage and wharfage charges at Galveston.

The banking facilities for handling the business of the city, are ample.

With five National banks, showing $1,671,000 capital and surplus, [see reports of March 5th, 1895], and $2,400,000 deposits, and two private banks with large capital, all legitimate business demands can be accommodated.

Our Clearing House reports show for the past six months, the volume of business to have reached $156,597,191, a weekly average of $6,138,354.

Nine Building and Loan Associations afford assistance to all desiring an opportunity of owning their own dwellings, on easy terms, and the many residences erected during the last five years, show that our people are strong in the belief that "there is no place like home."

The area of the city proper, is nine square miles. Surrounding it are "additions" so well built up as to seem part of the city.

Houston's population in 1890, according to the United States census, was 27,411. The population in 1894, according to the Directory, [based on 3 persons for each name in it], was 61,530.

The population of the "additions" reaches at least 5 per cent. of the city proper.

January 1st, the assessed value of the city was $22,463,185, of Harris county at the same date, it was $28,141,103.

The Houston City Street Railway [Electric line] with its forty miles of track, affords rapid access to all parts of the city and suburbs.

A reference to the pages following, will give some information as to the "places in the city," and "how to reach them."

"THE BELT."

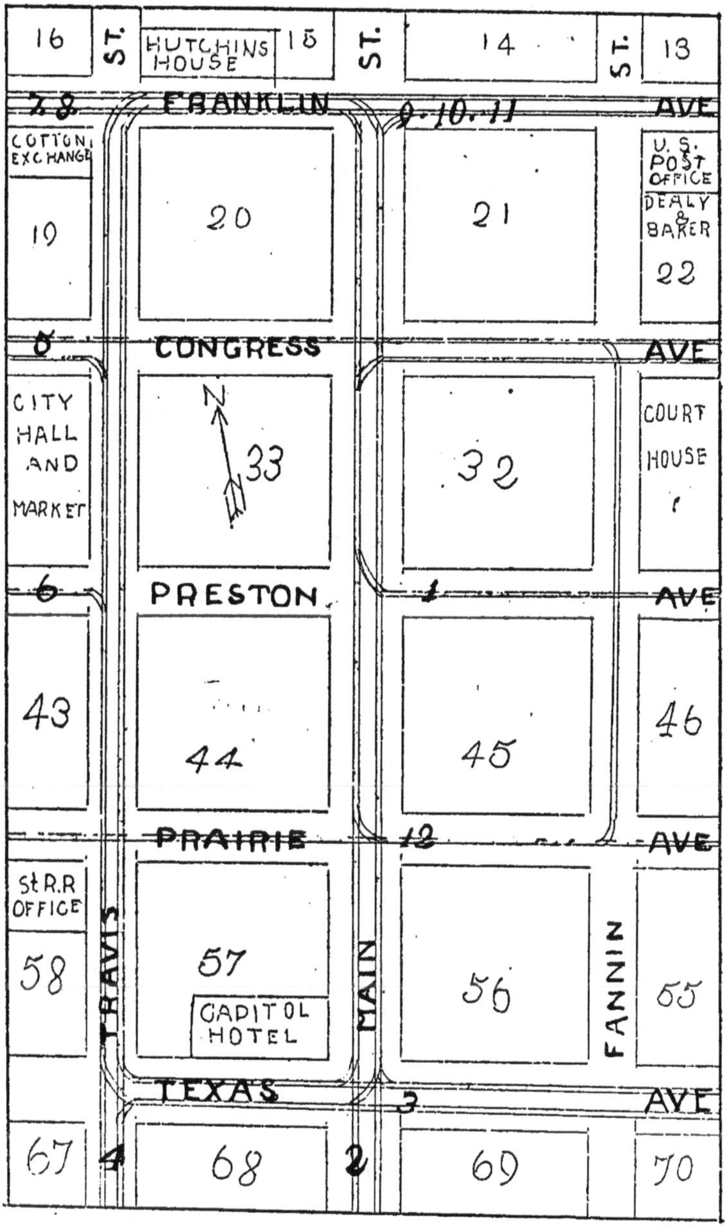

On Franklin avenue from Travis to Main.
On Main street from Franklin avenue to Texas avenue.
On Texas avenue from Main to Travis streets.
On Travis street from Texas avenue to Franklin avenue.
☞All cars, except Route No. 6, pass on around the Belt.

STREET CAR ROUTES.

CARS LEAVE STANDS AS FOLLOWS:

No. 1—Congress, Preston and Main,
Every 9 minutes after 5:10 a. m.
No. 2.—Fannin, Travis and Main,
On the hour and every 15 minutes thereafter.
No. 3.—LaBranche, Caroline and Main,
On the hour and every 15 minutes thereafter.
No. 4.—Louisiana and Main,
On the hour and every 20 minutes thereafter.
No. 5.—San Felipe and Main,
On the hour and every 15 minutes thereafter.
No. 6.—Houston Avenue and First Ward,
On the hour and every 30 minutes thereafter.
No. 7.—Glenwood, Grand Central Depot and Main,
On the hour and every 10 minutes thereafter.
No. 8.—Houston Heights, Grand Central Depot and Main,
On the hour and every 20 minutes thereafter.
No. 9.—Liberty Avenue and Fifth Ward,
On the hour and every 15 minutes thereafter.
No. 10.—Montgomery Avenue and Fifth Ward,
Every 40 minu'es after 5:40 a. m.
No. 11.—Franklin Avenue, Volksfest Park and Main,
On the hour and every 25 minutes thereafter.
No. 12.—Aransas Pass Depot and Third Ward,
On the hour and every 15 minutes thereafter.

For convenience, the starting point of all the following lines is made at the corner of Main street and Congress avenue, which point all the cars in the city pass, except as otherwise noted.

In taking a car for any line, please note sign on car, which is given below, in italics, as neither the lights or colors of the cars will serve for a guide, at present.

Note the "No." attached to each route, as reference in other parts of this guide, is made by Route No.

No. 1.—Congress, Preston and Main Streets:

South on Main to Texas avenue, west on Texas avenue to Travis, North on Travis to Franklin, east on Franklin to Main, south on Main to Preston, east on Preston to St. Charles, north on St. Charles to Congress, west on Congress to starting point.

☞ Take this car for G., C. & S. F., I. & G. N. and G., H. & H. depots.

No. 2.—Fannin, Travis and Main Streets:

South on Main to Capitol, east on Capitol to Fannin, south on Fannin to McGowan, west on McGowan to Travis, north on Travis to Franklin, east on Franklin to Main, south on Main to starting point.

☛ Take this car for the "Auditorium."

No. 3.—LaBranch, Caroline and Main Streets:

North on Main to Franklin, west on Franklin to Travis, south on Travis to Texas avenue, east on Texas avenue to LaBranch, south on LaBranch to Pease, east on Pease to Jackson, south on Jackson to Pierce, west on Pierce to Caroline, north on Caroline to Texas avenue, west on Texas avenue to Main, north on Main to starting point.

☛ Take this car for the Emancipation Grounds.

No. 4.—Louisiana and Main Streets:

North on Main to Franklin, west on Franklin to Travis, south on Travis to Capitol, west on Capitol to Louisiana, south on Louisiana to Hadley, returns by same streets to Capitol, east on Capitol to Main, north on Main to starting point.

☛ Take this car for Fair Ground addition and connection with Tuam and Fairview avenue cars. It also goes within three blocks of the Auditorium.

No. 5.—San Felipe and Main Streets:

West on Congress to Milam, south on Milam to Rusk, west on Rusk to Smith, south on Smith to Polk, on Polk to Robin, southwest on Robin to Heiner, south on Heiner to Andrews, southwest on Andrews to Wilson, north on Wilson to San Felipe, northeast on San Felipe to Dallas, east on Dallas to Milam, north on Milam to Prairie, east on Prairie to Fannin, north on Fannin to Congress, west on Congress to starting point.

☛ Take this car for City, Hebrew and Springfield Cemeteries.

No. 6.—Houston Avenue and First Ward:

[This car starts from corner Travis street and Preston avenue.] West on Preston avenue to Washington, west on Washington to Houston avenue, north on Houston avenue to Crockett—returns over same streets to starting point.

☛ Take this car for Beauchamp's Springs and Bayland Orphan Home.

No. 7.—Glenwood, Grand Central Depot and Main Street:

North on Main to Franklin, west on Franklin to Fifth, north on Fifth to Washington, west on Washington to Chaneyville, returning east on Washington to Fifth, south on Fifth to Louisiana and Congress, east on Congress to Travis, south on Travis to Texas avenue, east on Texas avenue to Main, north on Main to starting point.

☛ Take this car to Grand Central Depot, Glenwood and German Cemeteries, National and Southern Cotton-Oil Mills.

No 8.—Houston Heights:

Route same as No. 7 to Glenwood, thence west on Washington street to Houston Heights, returning to Glenwood, thence as Route No. 7 to starting point.

☛ Passes Grand Central Depot, Glenwood and German Cemeteries, National, Southern and Consumers' Cotton-Oil Mills, H. & T. C. Shops, Coombs' Park, KNIGHTS OF PYTHIAS ENCAMPMENT GROUNDS, and connects with the Bruner Addition cars. The United States Mails carried on these cars.

No. 9.—Liberty Avenue, 5th Ward, and Main Street:

North on Main to Franklin, east on Franklin to San Jacinto, north on San Jacinto to Willow, north on Willow to Liberty, on Liberty to Third, on Third to Nance, on Nance to Hill, on Hill to Bremond, on Bremond to Odin avenue, on Odin avenue to Conti, on Conti to McKee, on McKee to Liberty, on Liberty to Willow, on Willow to San Jacinto, on San Jacinto to Franklin, on Franklin to Travis, on Travis to Texas avenue, on Texas avenue to Main, on Main to starting point.

☛ This car nearest route to Merchants and Planters' Oil Mill, Dickson Car-Wheel works, Southern Pacific shops, T. & N. O., and G., H. & S. A., H. E. & W. T. and M., K. & T. freight depots, Bayou City, Cleveland and Union Compresses, and Houston Driving Park.

No. 10.—Montgomery Avenue, 5th Ward and Main Street:

North on Main to Franklin, east on Franklin to San Jacinto, North on San Jacinto to Willow north on Willow to Wood, on Wood to Montgomery avenue, on Montgomery avenue to Hogan, returning by same route to Willow, on Willow to San Jacinto, on San Jacinto to Franklin, on Franklin to Travis, on Travis to Texas avenue, on Texas avenue to Main, on Main to starting point.

☛ Take this car for M., K. & T., H., E. & W. T.; T. & N. O., and G., H. & S. R'y depots.

No. 11.—Franklin Avenue and Volksfest:

North on Main to Franklin avenue, east on Franklin avenue to Jackson, on Jackson to Magnolia, on Magnolia to Chartres, on Chartres to German, on German to Palmer, on Palmer to Engelke, on Engelke to Sampson, (Volksfest Park) returns by same streets to Travis, south on Travis to Texas avenue, east on Texas avenue to Main, north on Main to starting point.

☛ Take this line for Volksfest Park and the Catholic Cemetery.

No. 12.—Aransas Pass Depot and 3d Ward:

South on Main to Prairie avenue, east on Prairie avenue to Hamilton, south on Hamilton to Lamar, east on Lamar to Hutchins, south on Hutchins to Pease, west on Pease to Jackson, north on Jackson to Texas avenue, west on Texas avenue to Travis, north on Travis to Franklin avenue, east on Franklin to Main, south on Main to starting point.

Milby & Dow Building.

RAILROADS.

Galveston Houston & Henderson Railroad—I. & G. N. operating.

Gulf Colorado & Santa Fe R'y—General offices in Galveston.

Galveston Harrisburg & San Antonio R'y—see S. P. Co., Atlantic System.

Galveston La Porte & Houston R'y—J. Waldo, President; T. W. Ford, 1st Vice-President and Gen'l Attorney; C. W. Hammit, 2d Vice-President and Gen'l Manager; Isaac Heffron, 3d Vice-President, and Ass't Gen'l Manager; T. J. Boyles, Treasurer; C. W. Nelson, Auditor and Gen'l Freight, Ticket and Passenger agent; J. H. Tennant, Secy; J. H. Taylor, Supt.; F. H. Peters, Chief Engineer; M. W. Wambough, Ass't Engineer. April 1st, General offices will be in Mason Building, corner of Main and Rusk streets.

Houston East & West Texas R'y—E. S. Jamison, President; M. G. Howe, Vice-President and Gen'l Manager; H. Downey, Gen'l Freight and Passenger agent; N. S. Meldrum, Secretary and Treasurer; E. Dargan, Auditor; Thos. Cronin, Superintendent. General offices corner of Wood and Walnut streets, Fifth Ward.

Houston & Texas Central Railroad—General offices over Grand Central Depot, Washington avenue, Thos. H. Hubbard, President; G. A. Quinlan, Vice-President; E. W. Cave, Secretary and Treasurer; Geo. Kidd, Auditor; C. W. Bein, Traffic Manager; H. A. Jones, G. F. A.; M. L. Robbins, G. P. A.; W. L. Westcott, R. W. Agent; W. S. Napier, Gen'l Bag. Agent.

International & Great Northern Railroad—General offices in Palestine.

Missouri Kansas & Texas R'y—General offices in Texas, at Denison.

Texas & New Orleans Railroad—see So. Pacific Co., Atlantic System.

Texas Transportation Co.—see Southern Pacific Co., Atlantic System.

Texas Western R'y—General offices Burns' building, corner Main and Prairie, Si. Packard, Receiver, E. A. Campbell, General Manager.

Southern Pacific Co., Atlantic System—General offices 1109½ Franklin avenue, J. Kruttschnitt, General Manager; W. G. Van Vleck, General Superintendent; C. B. Seger, Secretary and Auditor; Paul Flato, Treasurer.

C. C. Gibbs, Land Commissioner, San Antonio.

C. W. Bein, TrafficManager; H. A. Jones, Gen'l Freight Agent; L. J. Parks, As't Gen'l Passenger Agent, offices over Grand Central depot.

PASSENGER DEPOTS.

Grand Central Depot—Washington avenue, between Seventh and Eighth streets. Used by the Houston & Texas Central, Galveston Harrisburg & San Antonio, Gulf Colorado & Santa Fe, San Antonio & Aransas Pass, Texas & New Orleans, and New York Texas & Mexican Roads, W. F. Simmons, Ticket Agent. Routes Nos. 7 and 8.

Gulf Colorado & Santa Fe Depot—corner Congress and St. Emanuel streets, D. M. Field, Ticket Agent. Route No. 1.

Galveston Houston & Henderson R'd—Schrimpf, between Congress and Franklin, G. D. Hunter, Ticket Agent. Route No. 1.

Galveston LaPorte & Houston—corner San Jacinto and Commerce, ————, Ticket Agent. Routes Nos. 9, 10 and 11.

Houston East & West Texas Depot—corner Wood and Walnut, Fifth Ward, Sam'l C. Timpson, Ticket Agent. Routes Nos. 9 and 10.

Missouri Kansas & Texas Depot—Second and Girard streets, R. B. Courtney, Ticket Agent. Route No. 10.

S. A. & A. P. R'y—trains leave from Grand Central Depot, W. F. Simmons, Ticket Agent. Routes Nos. 7and 8.

I. & G. N. R'd Depot—Schrimpf, between Congress and Franklin avenues, G. D. Hunter, Ticket Agent. Route No. 1.

S. P. Co., Atlantic System—see Grand Central Depot.

Union Depot—used by I. & G. N. and G. H. & H. Roads. Route No. 1.

Texas Western R'y Depot—Commerce and St. Emmanuel, J. M. Swisher, Ticket Agent. Route No. 1.

CITY TICKET OFFICES.

H. & T. C., T. & N. O., G. H. & S. A., S. A. & A. P., N. Y. T. & M.,	No. 207 Main street, R. E. George, Ticket Agent. E. Hartman, As't Ticket Ag't.

M. K. & T., No. 211 Main street, R. B. Courtney, Ticket Agent.

I. & G. N., 911 Franklin avenue, G. D. Hunter, Ticket Agent.

Mallory Line Steam Ships—M. Raphael, Agent, No. 914½ Franklin avenue.

FREIGHT DEPOTS.

Galveston Houston & Henderson R'd—Schrimpf, between Congress and Franklin. Route No. 1.

Galveston LaPorte & Houston R'y—corner San Jacinto and Commerce. Routes No. 9, 10 and 11.

Galveston Harrisburg & San Antonio, and Texas & New Orleans R'ds—Fifth Ward, on line of T. & N. O. road, near crossing Montgomery avenue. Routes Nos. 9 and 10.

International & Great Northern R'd—same as G. H. & H. Route Nos. 1.

Houston East & West Texas R'y—Wood street, near Walnut. Routes No. 9 and 10.

Houston & Texas Central R'd—corner Washington and Fifth streets. Routes No. 7 and 8.

Missouri Kansas & Texas R'y—Fifth Ward. Montgomery avenue and Collins street. Route No. 10.

San Antonio & Aransas Pass R'y—Lamar and West Broadway. Route No. 12.

HOUSTON DIRECT NAVIGATION CO.

Office—Franklin avenue, No. 1109½. L. Megget, Superintendent. Operates Freight line between Houston and Galveston, on Buffalo Bayou.

STEAMBOATS.

Steamer Eugene, Fred. Allien, Master, carrying passengers and United States Mails, leaves for Lynchburg, Baytown, Morgan's Point, Bayview and La Porte, on Monday, Wednesday and Friday, at 9:30 a. m., sharp. Returning, leaves La Porte on Tuesday, Thursday and Saturday, at 8:00 a. m., arriving at Houston, at 3 p. m.

RAILROAD SHOPS.

Houston & Texas Central R'd. S. R. Tuggles, S. M. P. & M.; Chas. Burns, M. M.; Jas. McGee, M. C. B.

Machine Shops—First Ward, north of the railroad track, west side of Houston avenue.

Car Shops—North side of railroad track, west side of White street.

Creosote—Back of Car shops. Routes Nos. 7 and 8.

Southern Pacifie Co., Fifth Ward. J. J. Ryan, M. M.; J. R. Cade, General Foreman. North side of railroad track, between McKee and Montgomery. Creosote Works—On line of railroad, one mile east of city. Route No. 9.

Houston East & West Texas R'y—Fifth Ward, Maffit street, between Second and Third. Route No. 9.

EXPRESS COMPANIES.

American Express Co.—Office No. 1007, Franklin avenue, C. W. Taylor, Agent.

Pacific Express Co.—Office No. 909 Franklin avenue, (under Hutchins House), Geo. A. Riley, Agent.

Texas Express Co.—Office and Agent same as Pacific Express.

Wells, Fargo & Co.'s Express—Office corner Fannin street and Franklin avenue, A. Christeson, Superintendent; J. L. Dean, Agent. (Office also at Grand Central Depot.)

MASONIC TEMPLE.

HALLS AND PUBLIC BUILDINGS.

Auditorium—corner Main and McGowen streets. Route No. 2.

Bayland Orphan Home—Beauchamp Spring road northwest two miles. Route No. 6.

Bell's Hall—Fifth Ward, 1114 Liberty avenue. Route No. 9.

DePelchin Faith Home—Chenevert street, between Calhoun and Pierce avenues. Route No. 3.

Elks' Hall—No. 1008½ Prairie avenue. All Routes.

Harris County Jail—corner Caroline street and Preston avenue. Route No. 1.

Harris County Court House—Congress, Preston, Fannin and San Jacinto. Routes Nos. 1 and 12 pass—all other routes within one block.

Houston City Hall and Market House—Fronts, Travis street. between Congress and Preston avenues. All routes pass.

Houston Cotton Exchange and Board of Trade—corner Travis street and Franklin avenue. All routes pass.

Houston Light Guard Armory—corner Texas avenue and Fannin. Routes Nos. 3 and 12.

Houston Lyceum—Hall and Library, north wing of City Hall, second floor. All routes pass.

Houston Postoffice—corner Franklin avenue and Fannin street. Routes Nos. 9, 10 and 11.

Knights of Pythias Hall—Burns building, corner Main and Prairie. All routes pass.

Masonic Temple—corner Main street and Capitol avenue. Routes Nos. 3 and 4 pass—all others within one block.

Odd Fellows Hall—Mason building, corner Main and Rusk. All routes pass within two blocks.

Sweeny & Coombs Opera House—Fannin, between Congress and Preston avenues. All cars pass within one block.

Turners Hall—corner Prairie and Caroline. Route 1 within one block.

Y. M. C. Association—Texas Avenue, between Main and Fannin. All routes within half block.

BANKS AND BANKERS.

Commercial National—northeast corner Main street and Franklin avenue, W. B. Chew, President; R. A. Giraud, Cashier; G. A. Price, As't Cash'r.

First National—southeast corner Main street and Franklin avenue, A. P. Root, President; W. H. Palmer, Cashier; W. E. Hertford, As't Cash'r.

Houston National—northwest corner Main street and Congress avenue, Henry S. Fox, President; N. S. Munger, Cashier.

Planters and Mechanics' National—No. 213 Main street, between Congress and Franklin avenues. T. J. Boyles, President; O. C. Drew, Cashier; A. S. Vandervoort, Assistant Cashier.

South Texas National—southwest corner Main street and Franklin avenue, M. T. Jones, President; J. E. McAshan, Cashier; Ennis Cargill, Assistant Cashier.

Private Bank—T. W. House, Banker, No. 203 Main street, S. M. McAshan, Cashier; T. C. Dunn, Assistant Cashier.

Private Bankers—Sweeney & Fredericks, 316 Main street.

HOUSTON CLEARING HOUSE,

No. 913½ Franklin avenue, E. Raphael, Manager. Composed of Commercial National, First National, Houston National, Planters & Mechanics' National, South Texas National banks, and T. W. House, private banker. Clearances from September 1, 1894, to March 1, 1895, averaged over $1,000,000 per day.

BUILDING AND LOAN ASSOCIATIONS.

Acme Building and Loan Association—R. D. Gribble, President; M. A. Grant, Secretary. Office, Room 316, Kiam building.

Bayou City Building and Loan Association—A. K. Taylor, President; M. Kattman, Sec'y. Office, corner Main street and Franklin avenue.

Houston Land and Trust Company—W. B. Chew, President; Rufus Cage, Secretary. Office, corner Main street and Franklin avenue.

Inter-State Building and Loan Association—Chas. Stewart, President; O. M. Doty, Sec'y. Office, Room 200, Mason building.

Mechanics' Building and Loan Association—J. R. Cade, President; W. B. Munson, Sec'y. Office, 1007½ Congress avenue.

Magnolia Loan and Building Association—Ben. Kiam, President; Felix Haas, Sec'y. Office, Room 503, Kiam building.

Mutual Building and Loan Association—D.C.Smith, President; P. H. Galligher, Secretary. Office, No. 1009½ Congress avenue.

National Railway Building and Loan Association—J. M. Lee, President; G. H. Windle, Secretary. Office, 1016½ Congress avenue.

South Texas Loan and Building Association—A. Christeson, President; A. K. Taylor, Secretary. Office, Cotton Exchange.

Texas Savings, Real Estate and Investment Association—E. L. Dennis, President; M. Kattman, Secretary. Office, corner Main street and Franklin avenue.

Houston Cotton Exchange and Board of Trade.

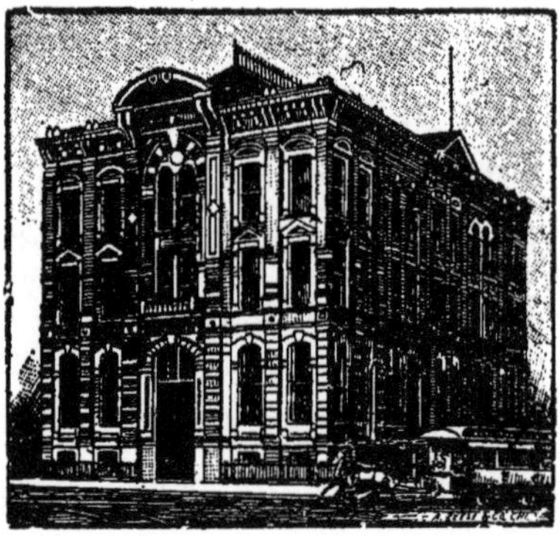

Building southwest cor. Travis street and Franklin avenue, H. W. Garrow, President; George W. Kidd, Secretary. All cars pass this corner.

HOUSTON BUSINESS LEAGUE.

Office, Room 200, Kiam building, northwest corner Main street and Preston avenue; James M. Cotton, President; W. W. Dexter, Secretary.

CHAIRMEN OF COMMITTEES.

Finance—H. T. Keller; Excursions—H. T. D. Wilson; Conventions—R. M. Johnson; Membership—Robt. Adair; Industries. etc.—S. T. Swinford; Railroads, etc.—S. W. Sydnor; Immigration—Tom. Richardson; Local Entertainments—Clifford Grunewald; Public Comfort—R. B. Morris; Advertising and Printing—G. J. Palmer; Texas Products—W. B. Slosson; Navigation—Mose Raphael; Statistics —D. Bryan; Audits—Arthur Lipper.

Houston Club.

Rooms in Mason building, between Main stree and Rusk avenue; O. T. Holt, President; J Kruttschnitt, Vice President; L. J. Parks, Secretary and Treasurer. General Business Committee—Chas. Dillingham, George A. Cragin, John F. Dickson.

Houston Light Guard Club.

Rooms at Light Guard Armory, corner Texas avenue and Fannin street.

Auditorium.

Northeast corner Main street and McGowen avenue. In course of construction—will be ready for use at the Confederate Veterans' re-union. Route No. 2.

Western Union Telegraph Co.

Office, No. 117 Main street, between Franklin and Commerce avenues. Geo. C. Felton, Manager.

MUNICIPAL GOVERNMENT.

Mayor--John T. Browne, office south wing City Hall, second floor. Hours, 9 to 10 a. m.

Secretary--A. S. Richardson, office south wing City Hall, second floor. Hours, 9 a. m. to 1 p. m., and 3 to 6 p. m.

Assistant Secretary--B. R. Warner, office and hours, same as Secretary.

Assessor and Collector--Justin C. White, office north wing City Hall, second floor. Hours, 9 to 12 and 1 to 5 p. m.

Recorder—W. B. Hill, office over Police Station, Louisiana, between Congress and Preston avenues.

City Attorney--John Stewart, office 304½ Main street.

City Marshal—James H. Pruett, office at Police Station, Louisiana street.

Deputy Marshal--J. M. Ray.

Day Clerk--M. T. Forrest.

Night Clerk--M. Monighan.

Office at Police Station, Louisiana street between

Congress and Preston avenues. One of the above officers can be seen at all hours, day or night.

Health Officer—Dr. G. W. Larendon, office 315½ Main street.

Health Inspector—S. W. Proctor, office at Police Station.

Scavenger—Jas. A. Thompson, office at Police Station.

Market Master—A. R. Miller, office at City Market, ground floor.

Superintendent of Public Schools—Prof. W. S. Sutton, office south wing City Hall. Hours, Fridays, 11 a. m. to 12 m., other days, 3 to 4:30 p. m.

Chief of Fire Department—Thos. S. Ravell, office City Hall, second floor.

Assistant Chief—Fred Kersten, office City Hall, second floor.

ALDERMEN.

First Ward—L. Sonnen, W. J. Kohlhauff.
Second Ward—W. G. Heinze, Hy. Freund.
Third Ward—Jules Hirsch, Si Packard.
Fourth Ward—W. H. Bailey, B. Repsdorph.
Fifth Ward—Jas. McAughan, W. J. Aubertin.

CHAIRMEN OF STANDING COMMITTEES.

Finance—Jules Hirsch; Streets and Bridges—Jas. McAughan; Markets—Hy. Freund; Police—L. Sonnen; Journals—W. G. Heinze; Fire Department—W. J. Kohlhauff; Ordinances—W. H. Bailey; Hospitals—B. Repsdorph; Public Lights—W. J.

Aubertin; Public Schools—Si Packard; Sewers—W. J. Aubertin.

Board of Appraisement—Hy. Freund, W. J. Kohlhauff, of Board of Aldermen, and Robt. Adair.

Board Trustees Public Schools—Rufus Cage, C. Lombardi, A. J. Jourde, J. O. Carr, E. Raphael, E. P. Hamblen.

The City Council meets in regular session at their chamber in the south wing of the City Hall, each Monday in the month, at 4 p. m.

FIRE DEPARTMENT.

Chief—Thomas F. Ravell, office at City Hall, second floor.

Protection Hose Co. No. 1—Foreman, H. Damuth, 612 Fannin street.

Hook and Ladder No. 1—Foreman, Fred DeLesdernier, Central Fire Station, corner Prairie and San Jacinto streets.

Stonewall No. 3—Foreman, Tom O'Leary, 408 Smith street.

Chemical No. 4—Foreman, Frank Hays, Central Fire Station, corner San Jacinto and Prairie streets.

Steamer No. 5—Foreman, Wm. Loftus, Central Fire Station, corner San Jacinto and Prairie streets.

Mechanics No. 6—Foreman, Fred Erichson, 1106 Washington street.

Washington No. 8—Foreman, W. W. Thomas, Polk and Crawford.

Curtin No. 9—Foreman, Richard Abels, 910 Hardy street.

Seibert No. 10—Foreman, W. P. Seibert, Chartres street, near corner Franklin.

Aerial Truck.—Central Fire Station.

FIRE DISTRICTS.

First Ward—

No. 12—Milam and Commerce.
" 13—Washington and Seventh.
" 14—Houston and Edwards.
" 15—Houston and Crockett.
" 16—Waters-Pierce Oil Co.'s Warehouse.

Second Ward—

No. 21—Main and Congress.
" 23—Congress and Austin.
" 24—Franklin and St. Emanuel.
" 25—Congress and East Broadway.
" 26—German street and I. & G. N. Railroad crossing.
" 27—Chenevert and Magnolia.
" 28—Buffalo and Commerce.

Third Ward—

No. 31—Main and Capitol.
" 32—Main and McKinney.
" 34—Texas and LaBranch.
" 35—Congress and Chenevert.
" 36—Austin and McKinney.
" 37—Main and Pease.
" 312—Capitol and Jackson.
" 313—Bell and Louisiana.
" 314—Dallas and Jackson.
" 315—Chartres and McKinney.
" 316—McKinney and Broadway.
" 323—Jackson and Pease.
" 325—Gray and Austin.
" 326—Main and McGowan.

Fourth Ward, south—
No. 41—Main and Prairie.
" 42—Milam and Prairie.
" 43—Capitol and Louisiana.
" 45—Milam and McKinney.
" 46—Dallas and Smith.
" 47—San Felipe and Bagby.
" 412—San Felipe and Hopson.
" 413—Milam and Webster.
" 415—Milam and Clay.
" 416—Main and Leland.
" 421—Fair Ground Addition.
" 423—Si Packard's Laundry.

Fifth Ward—
No. 51—Willow and Allen.
" 52—Liberty and Third.
" 53—Montgomery Road.
" 54—Liberty and McKee.
" 56—Semmes and Providence.
" 57—Hardy and Opelousas.
" 512—Liberty and Carr.
" 513—Hardy and Waverly.
" 514—Montgomery Road.

Fourth Ward, north—
No. 61—Preston and Tenth.
" 62—Washington and John.
" 63—Lubbock and Sabine.
" 65—Henderson and Reisner.
" 67—Washington and Taylor.

CHIEF'S SIGNALS.

2 Taps—More Pressure.
1 Tap—Fire out, turn off Pressure.
111—111—111—GENERAL ALARM.

HOUSTON HIGH SCHOOL.

E. T. Heiner, Architect

PUBLIC SCHOOLS.

SUPERINTENDENT—W. S. SUTTON.

Board of Trustees—John T. Browne, President; E. Raphael, Secretary; C. Lombardi, J. O. Carr, E. P. Hamblen, A. J. Jourde.

Board of Examiners—W. S. Sutton, G. Duvernoy, T. J. Pattillo.

LOCATION OF SCHOOL BUILDINGS.

High School—(New building in course of construction. Value, $100,000).

High School—Kiam building on Congress avenue, opposite Court House, T. G. Harris, Principal. Reached by Route No. 1; all other routes pass within one block.

Market House School—City Hall, second floor; T. V. Kirk, Principal. All routes pass City Hall.

Longfellow School—(Third Ward), corner Chartres street and Bell avenue, T. J. Pattillo, Principal. Routes Nos. 3 and 12.

Fannin Street School—(Third Ward), corner Fannin street and McGowan avenue, T. B. McDonough, Principal. Route No. 2.

Taylor School—(Fourth Ward, South), corner Milam street and Clay avenue, R. N. Little, Principal. Routes Nos. 2 and 4.

Dow School—(Fourth Ward, North), T. J. Atwood, Principal. Routes Nos. 7 and 8.

Houston Avenue School—(First Ward), Houston avenue and Bingham street, W. A. de LaMatyr, Principal. Route No. 6.

Hamilton Street School—(Second Ward), Hamilton street, between Commerce and Magnolia avenues, S. D. Magers, Principal. Routes Nos. 1 and 11.

Elysian Street School—(Fifth Ward), Elysian street, between Eagle and Liberty avenues, W. W. Barnett, Principal. Route No. 9.

Cascara School—(Fifth Ward), Lorraine street, between McKee and Hardy streets. J. E. Niday, Principal. Route No. 9.

First Ward Colored School—corner Bingham and Colorado streets, A. R. Anderson, Principal. Route No. 6.

Second Ward Colored School—German street, between Buffalo street and I. & G. N. R'd, S. H. Crawford, Principal. Routes Nos. 1 and 11.

Third Ward Colored School—Jackson street and Calhoun avenue, S. C. Collins, Principal. Routes Nos. 3 and 12.

Fourth Ward Colored School—corner State and Trinity streets, W. S. Francis, Principal. Routes Nos. 7 and 8.

Fifth Ward Colored School—corner Bremond and Conti streets, W. B. Cogle, Principal. Route No. 9.

Colored High School—(Fourth Ward, South). San Felipe street, corner Bagby street, Chas. Atherton, Principal. Route No. 5.

Value of school property—outside of the High School building, $237,175.

OPEN ALL DAY.

911 CONGRESS AVE.

PAUL WEBER. PALACE MEAT MARKET.

Fresh Vegetables, Butter and Eggs. Choice Meat.

FREE DELIVERY.

Call on E. M. BURKE,

—FOR—

LIME, Portland and Rosendale CEMENTS

Plaster Paris, Hair, Fibre, Laths, Fire Brick, Fire Clay, Land Plaster, Garden Tile, Common Brick, San Jacinto Sand.

SEWER PIPE ALL SIZES.

Agent ROYAL CEMENT PLASTER.

Telephone No. 37. 814 Commerce Avenue.

HOUSTON, TEXAS.

FIRST PRESBYTERIAN CHURCH.

CHURCHES.

BAPTIST.

Baptist Mission—Washington avenue. Routes No. 7 and 8.

First Baptist Church—northeast corner Rusk and Fannin. Route No. 2 passes; all other routes pass within three blocks.

German Baptist Church—23 Clay street, Fourth Ward, North. Routes Nos. 6, 7 and 8.

Second Baptist Church—Fifth Ward, corner Hardy street and Liberty avenue. Route No. 8.

CATHOLIC.

Church of the Annunciation—corner Texas avenue and Crawford street. Route No. 3.

St. Joseph's Chapel—northeast corner Franklin and Caroline. Route No. 11.

St. Joseph's Church—southwest corner Houston and Kane. Routes Nos. 6, 7 and 8.

St. Patrick's Church—southeast corner Conti and Maury streets. Route No. 9.

CHRISTIAN.

Central Christian Church—northwest corner Caroline and Capitol. Route No. 3.

North Side Christian Church—southeast corner Summer and White. Route Nos. 7 and 8.

EPISCOPAL.

Christ Church—northeast corner Texas avenue and Fannin street. Route No. 3.

Clemens Memorial of the Good Shepherd—corner Sabine and Bingham. Routes Nos. 6, 7 and 8.

St. Mary's Church—northeast corner Hardy and Conti streets. Route No. 9.

St. John's Chapel of Christ Church—northwest corner Velasco and Leeland streets. Routes Nos. 3 and 12.

Trinity Chapel of Christ Church—Fair Ground Addition. Route No. 4.

HEBREW.

Tempel Beth Israel—Synagogue southeast corner Crawford street and Franklin avenue. Route No. 11.

LUTHERAN.

First German Evangelical Lutheran Church—southeast corner Texas avenue and Milam street. Route No. 5.

German Lutheran Trinity Church—west side Louisiana street, between Preston and Prairie avenues. Route No 6.

METHODIST.

First German M. E. Church, South—northeast corner McKinney avenue and Milam street. Route No. 5.

German M. E. Church—corner Union and Hemphill streets. Routes Nos. 7 and 8.

McAshan Chapel M. E. Church, South—corner Buffalo and German streets. Route No. 11.

McKee Street M.E. Church—east side McKee street, between Providence and Conti. Route No. 9.

Mission M. E. Church—San Felipe road near Southern Pacific R'y crossing. Route No. 5.

Shearn Memorial M. E. Church, South—north side Texas avenue, between Travis and Milam streets. All routes pass within half block.

Tabernacle M. E. Church, South--No. 1217 Polk avenue, corner Caroline street. Route No. 3.

Washington Street M. E. Church, South--No. 1513, Washington street, between Clay and Trinity streets. Routes Nos. 7 and 8.

PRESBYTERIAN.

First Presbyterian Church--Capitol avenue, between Main and Travis. Route No. 4 passes; all other routes within one square.

Hardy Street Mission--Hardy street, between Lorain and Noble. Route No. 9.

Lubbock Street Presbyterian Church--Lubbock street, between Sabine and Silver. Routes Nos. 7 and 8.

Second Presbyterian Church—corner Lamar avenue and Crawford street. Routes Nos. 3 and 12.

Second Ward Mission—corner Magnolia and Hamilton. Routes Nos. 1 and 11.

SALVATION ARMY.

Salvation Army Barracks—Milam street, between Preston and Prairie aves. Routes Nos. 5 and 6

COLORED DENOMINATIONS.

Antioch Missionary Baptist Church—313 Robin. Route No 5.

Bethel Missionary Baptist Church—corner Andrews and Crosby. Route No. 5.

Boynton Chapel M. E. Church—corner Paige and Dallas avenue. Routes Nos. 3 and 12.

Brown's Chapel A. M. E. Church—Washington, between Court and Weichman. Routes Nos. 7 and 8.

Burton Grove Missionary Baptist Church—Kessler street, between Ninth and Tenth. Routes Nos. 6, 7 and 8.

Camp Zion Baptist Church—Pless, Engelke and A. Route No. 11.

Damascus Baptist Church—Chaneyville. Routes Nos. 7 and 8.

Goodhope Missionary Baptist Church—corner Saulnier and Wilson. Route No. 5.

Jerusalem Missionary Baptist Church—Hutchins, between McGowan and Tuam avenues. Route No. 12.

Jordan Grove Missionary Baptist Church—2015 Dowling street. Route No. 12.

Macedonia Baptist Church—corner Shearn and Beach. Route No. 6.

Mount Calvary Baptist Church—northeast corner Texas avenue and Live Oak. Route No. 3.

Mount Pillar Baptist Church—corner Hemphill and Lubbock. Route Nos. 7 and 8.

Mount Pleasant Baptist Church—2714 Liberty avenue. Route No. 9.

Mount Vernon M. E. Church—Vine, between Shea and New Orleans avenues. Route No. 10.

Mount Zion Missionary Baptist Church—German, between I. & G. N., Place and Buffalo. Route No. 11.

Pleasant Grove Baptist Church—Grove, between Odin avenue and Orange. Route No. 9.

Sherman Chapel C. M. E. Church—corner Saulnier and Buckner. Route No. 5.

Shiloh Baptist Church—1207 McMillan. Route No. 9.

Sloan Street M. E. Church—corner Nance and Sydnor. Route No. 9.

St. James M. E. Church—corner Howard and Lion. Route No. 5.

St. Paul's A. M. E. Church—Edwards, between Colorado and Sabine. Routes. Nos. 7 and 8.

Trinity M. E. Church—corner Travis street and Bell avenue. Route No. 2.

Watts' Chapel, Fourth Missionary Baptist Church—corner Dowling and Lamar. Route. No. 12.

Wesley Chapel A. M. E. Church—corner Texas avenue and Chartres street. Route No. 12.

CEMETERIES.

Cemetery Beth Israel—corner San Felipe and Wilson. Route No. 5.

Catholic Cemetery—Buffalo and Alexander streets. Route No. 11.

Deutsche Gesellschaft Cemetery—Washington St., adjoining Glenwood on west side. Routes Nos. 7 and 8.

*Episcopal Cemetery—Bagby, between McKinney and Lamar avenues. Nearest route, No. 5.

Evergreen Cemetery—on Harrisburg road, 2 miles east of Union Depot. Route No. 1, nearest.

German Lutheran Cemetery—adjoining Glenwood Cemetery on east side. Routes Nos. 7 and 8.

Glenwood Cemetery—Washington street, city limit. Routes Nos. 7 and 8.

Hebrew Cemetery (congregation Adath Yesurim)—north side San Felipe, half mile west S. P. R'y. Route No. 5.

Hollywood Cemetery (Colored)—half mile northwest of Chaney Junction, Washington Road. Route No. 8.

Magnolia Cemetery—San Felipe street, two blocks west of S. P. R'y. Route No. 5.

*Masonic Cemetery (old)—same as Episcopal.

Masonic Burial Grounds—in Glenwood Cemetery.

Potter's Field (new City Cemetery)—on Buffalo Bayou, end of Timpson street. Route No. 5.

---

*Not now in general use.

PARKS.

Coombs' Park—Houston Heights. Route No. 8.

Emancipation Grounds (colored)—two miles southeast. Routes Nos. 3 and 12 nearest street cars.

Houston Driving Park—near T. & N. O. R'd, four miles north. Reached by T. & N. O. R'd and street car Route No. 9.

Merkel's Grove—adjoining Volksfest Grounds, east side. Route No. 11.

Magnolia Park—on Galveston, La Porte & Houston R'd, four miles east.

Vick's Park—Washington street, near entrance to Houston Heights Boulevard. Route No. 8.

Volksfest Ground—two miles east. Route No. 11.

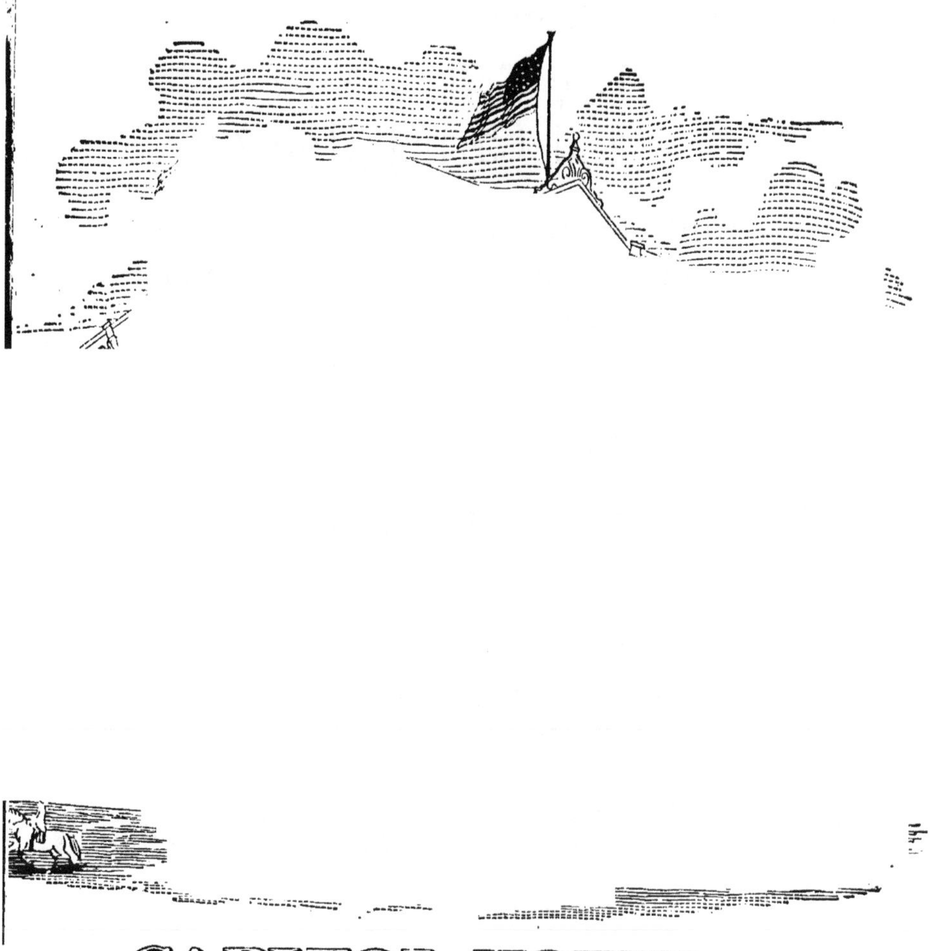

CAPITOL HOTEL,

PRINCIPAL HOTELS.

Avenue House—1807 Congress avenue, between Chenevert and Hamilton streets, Gus McKernon, Proprietor. Rates, $1 to $1.50 per day. Route No. 1.

Capitol Hotel—corner Main street and Texas avenue, G. McGinley, Proprietor. Rates, $2.50 to $3.50 per day. All cars pass this corner.

Grand Central Hotel—Washington street, opposite Grand Central Depot, James Lawlor, Proprietor. Rates, $2.50 to $3 per day. Routes Nos. 7 and 8.

Globe Hotel—corner Congress avenue and Austin street, Wm. Sullivan, Proprietor. Rates, $1 to $2 per day. Route No. 1.

Hotel Boyle—corner Louisiana and Congress avenue, W. T. Boyle, Proprietor. Rates $1.50 to $2 per day. Routes Nos. 7 and 8.

Florence Hotel—corner Wood and Willow streets, James E. Marti, Proprietor. Rates, $1 per day, $4 per week. Routes Nos. 9 and 10.

Fifth Ward Hotel—1206 Nance street, W. Colby, Proprietor. Rates, $1 per day. Route No. 9.

Logan House—Washington street, opposite Grand Central Depot. (Just completed).

King's Hotel—opposite I. & G. N. Depot, Congress avenue, No. 2315, K. K. King, Proprietor. Rates, $1 per day. Route No. 1.

Magnolia House—junction Washington and Preston avenue, Wm. Schultz, Proprietor. Rates, $1 per day. Routes Nos. 6, 7 and 8.

New Berry House—1413 Franklin avenue, S. L. Berry, Proprietor. Rates, $1 per day. Route No. 11.

New City Hotel—No. 2301 Congress avenue, John H. Quirk, Proprietor. Rates, $1 to $1 50 per day. Route No. 1.

New Dissen House—1010 Preston avenue, between Main and Fannin, L. D. Schaffer, Proprietor. Rates, $1.50 to $2. All routes within half block.

New Hutchins House—northeast corner Franklin and Travis. Kiber & Gueringer, Proprietors. Nates, $2, $2.50 and $3. All routes pass.

Rosenfield House—1304 Congress avenue, Mrs. C. C. O'Connor, Proprietor. Rates, $1 25 per day. Route No. 1.

Tremont House—corner Milam and Congress avenue, A. Sens, Proprietor. Rates $1.50 per day. Routes Nos 5, 7 and 8.

Washington House—1304 Washington street, Peter Moran, Proprietor. Rate, 75 cents per day. Routes Nos. 6, 7 and 8.

BOARDING HOUSES.

Mrs. Laura Alberts, No. 812 Travis street, $1.

Mrs. Laura Belknap, No. 115 San Jacinto St., $1.

Mrs. E. Angell, No. 509 San Jacinto street, $1.

Mrs. L. A. Bass, No 814 Main street, $1.

Mrs. Mary E. Campbell, No. 1009 Rusk avenue, $1.50 or $10 per week.

Mrs. M. B. Clement, No. 1211 Texas ave., $1.25.

Mrs. H. M. Dusenberry, corner Walker and Travis, $1 to $1.50.

Mrs. F. Gardener, No 710 Travis, $1.

Mrs. E. V. Gearing, No. 805 Main street, $1 meals only.

Mrs. J. R. Hooper, No. 1105 Providence, corner Chapman, $1.25 or $5 per week.

Mrs. F. B. Hite, No. 1104 Texas avenue, corner Fannin, $1 50 per day.

A. Key, No. 803 Main, $1.25.

Mrs. M. Marrast, No. 718 Main, $1.50 or $10 per week.

Miss Sallie Newsom, No. 810 Main, $2.

Mrs. L. J. Perkins, No. 912 Travis street, $1.50.

RESTAURANTS.

Big Casino—Clede & Kœnig, Proprietors, No. 908 Congress avenue.

Bon-Ton—B. A. Booth & Co., Proprietors, cor. Main and Prairie.

Colby's—Frank C. Colby, Proprietor, No. 408 Main street.

French Restaurant—Jake Chaure, Manager, No. 214 Main street.

Lunch Room—Muller & LeRoux, Proprietors, No. 912 Congress avenue.

New Idea—Gus A. Johnson, Proprietor, No. 1014 Prairie avenue.

PRINCETON—No. 1011 TEXAS AVENUE.

THE
NEW HUTCHINS HOUSE

COUNTY OFFICIALS.

All County Official have their Offices at the Court House, except as otherwise given below.

Judge Civil District Court—Sam. H. Brashear.

Clerk Civil District Court—J. R. Waties.

Judge Criminal District Court, Harris and Galveston Counties—E. D Cavin. Residence in Galveston Office in courthouse, during term of court.

Clerk Criminal District Court—George Ellis.

Criminal District Attorney—J. K. P. Gillaspie.

County Judge—J. G. Tod.

" Clerk—E. F. Dupree.

" Attorney—F. L. Schwander.

Sheriff—Albert Erichson.

County and State Collector of Taxes—Henry M. Curtin.

" Assessor—George H. Hermann.

" Treasurer—John Farmer.

" Surveyor—W. A. Polk.

County Superintendent of Public Instruction—B. L. James.

County Commissioner, Precinct No. 1—H. Baldwin Rice, Houston.

County Commissioner, Precinct No. 2—Howard Dunks, Crosby.

County Commissioner, Precinct No. 3—J. G. Ehrhardt, Westfield.

County Commissioner, Precinct No. 4—George E. Ollard, Hockley.

Justices Precinct No. 1—James T. Mahoney, 1108 Preston ave., James J. Hussey, 1205 Prairie ave.

Constable Precinct No. 1—W. W. Glass, 1901 Commerce ave.

TERMS OF COURT.

Civil District Court—first Mondays in February, April, June, October and December.

Criminal District Court—first Monday in January, March, May, July and November.

County Court—first Monday in January, March, May, July, September and November.

Justices Courts, Precinct No. 1—

Judge Mahoney, for Civil business—second Monday in each month; for Criminal business, daily, except Sunday.

Judge Hussey, for Civil business—last Monday in each month; for Criminal business, daily, except Sunday.

Gibbs Office Building

Compo Board Factory, Houston Heights.

Residence, Houston Heights.

MISCELLANEOUS.

INFIRMARIES.

Houston Infirmary—No. 1008 Washington street, corner Tenth, Drs. Stuart & Boyles, Proprietors; Dr. Joe Stuart, House Surgeon. Routes: Nos. 6, 7 and 8.

St. Joseph's Infirmary—Caroline and Franklin, under charge of the Sisters of Charity of the Incarnate Word. Route No. 11.

CAR WHEEL WORKS.

Dickson Car Wheel Works—Steam Mill and Pine streets, Fifth Ward. Routes Nos. 9 and 10.

COMPRESSES.

Bayou City Compress—north side Buffalo Bayou, between McKee and Maury. Route No. 9.

Cleveland Compress—east side Hill street on Buffalo Bayou, Fifth Ward. Route No. 9.

Inman Compress—north side H. & T. C. R'd, west city limits Routes Nos. 7 and 8.

New Press—Fifth Ward, east city limits. Nearest Route No. 9.

OIL MILLS.

Consumers Oil Mills—Houston Heights. Crushing capacity, 250 tons seed per day. Route No. 8.

Merchants and Planters' Oil Mill—on bank of Bayou, Fifth Ward, east city limits. Crushing capacity, 200 tons seed per day. Route No. 9.

National Oil Mills—Chaney Junction, one mile

west of city. Crushing capacity, 400 tons seed per day. Routes Nos. 7 and 8.

Southern Cotton Oil Mills—on S. P. R'y (G. H. & S. A.), west of city limits. Crushing capacity, 350 tons seed per day. Routes Nos. 7 and 8.

PUBLIC LIBRARIES.

Houston Lyceum—Rooms at City Hall, north wing, second floor. Open from 1 to 5 o'clock p. m., daily.

Y. M. C. A. Rooms—Texas avenue, between Main and Fannin. Open from 9 a. m. to 10 p. m.

HOUSTON NEWSPAPERS.

MORNING PAPER.

Houston Post—Daily. Semi-Weekly, Mondays and Thursdays. Office, No. 1111 Congress avenue.

EVENING PAPERS.

Age—Daily except Sunday. Office, No. 1111 Franklin avenue.

Herald—Daily except Sunday. Office, corner Preston avenue and San Jacinto street.

Press—Daily except Sunday. Office, No. 503½ Main street.

WEEKLY PAPERS.

Deutsche Zeitung und Anzeiger—Issued every Thursday, M. Tiling, Proprietor. Office, 1015½ Preston street

Texas Emigrant and Railroader—Office Shaw building, corner Congress and San Jacinto

Texas Freeman—Issued every Saturday. Office, No. 905 Prairie avenue

Texas Trade Review—Issued every Saturday. Office, 1013 Franklin avenue.

Texas World--Issued every Saturday Office No. 105½ Main street.

Texas Harpoon—Issued every Saturday. Office 711 Main street.

MONTHLY PAPERS.

Texas Presbyterian--Issued monthly. Office 110 Main street.

POSTAL INFORMATION.

NEW POSTOFFICE BUILDING.

[DEALY & BAKER'S Printing office is adjoining this Building.]

Postoffice--corner Fannin street and Franklin avenue, D. C. Smith, Postmaster; E. C. Smith Assistant Postmaster. Routes Nos. 9, 10 and 1 pass. All other routes pass within one block. Se map of belt.

All officers and clerks of the Postoffice are on th first floor.

The Superintendent of City Mails has charge o the distribution of matter to the carriers. and can be communicated with through their window.

OFFICE HOURS.

General Delivery--8 a. m. to 5 p. m. and 6 to 7 p. m
Stamp Window--8 a. m. to 5 p. m
Money Order Window--9 a. m. to 5 p. m.
Registry Window--9 a m. to 5 p. m
Sundays, General Delivery--9 to 10 a. m.

DELIVERY BY LETTER CARRIERS.

Business Districts—8 and 10 a. m. and 5 p. m.
Residence Districts—8:30 a m. and 1:30 p m
Sundays, at office only, from 9 to 10 a m.

COLLECTIONS FROM BOXES.

Business Districts—6 to 7 a. m; 8 to 9 a. m.; 10 to 11 a. m.; 3:30 p m; 6 to 7 p m

Residence Districts—8:30 a. m. to 12 m and 2:30 to 4 p. m.

Sundays, at 5 and 7 p m only.

Mails close 30 minutes before leaving time of train.

LOCATION OF STREET MAIL BOXES.

District No 1—First Ward, J. W. Misher, carrier Travis and Congress, Milam and Congress, Franklin and Travis, Franklin and Main, Hutchins House

District No. 2—Third Ward, Chas Weiss, carrier. Fannin and Congress, Main and Congress, Main and Franklin.

District No 3—Third Ward, J. B. West, carrier. Congress and Chenevert, Chartres between Magnolia and Maple, German aud I & G. N. Place, Engelke and Grand avenue, I. & G. N. R'd Depot, Congress and St. Emanuel, Franklin and Hutchins, Magnolia and Chenevert.

District No 4—Third Ward, A. Kier, carrier. Main and Clay, Main and Jefferson, Travis and McGowen, Austin and Gray, Austin and Leland, Hamilton and Calhoun, Bell and Crawford, Bell and Jackson

District No 5—Fourth Ward, South, Tom Moore, carrier. Dallas and Smith, San Felipe and Bagby, Milam and Polk, San Felipe and Fuller, San Felipe and Valentine, Louisiana and Webster.

District No. 6—Fourth Ward, North, George Fromm, carrier. Washington and Stanley, Houston avenue and Edwards, Houston avenue, No.

1801, Center and Taylor, Washington avenue, N. 2020, Silver street No. 713, Washington avenue, No. 1809, Washington avenue No. 1517.

District No. 7—Fifth Ward, F. R. Fenn, carrier. Wood and Willow, Liberty and Walnut, New Orleans avenue and Walnut, Liberty and McKee, Providence and Elysian, Semmes and Odin avenue, Carr and Odin avenue, Odin avenue and Orange, Hill and Nance, Semmes and Nance, Hardy and New Orleans avenue.

District No. 8—Fourth Ward, South, J. J. Billow, carrier. Main and Preston, Main and Texas avenue, Preston and Travis, Preston and Milam, Preston and Louisiana.

District No. 9—Third Ward, H. T. Brock, carrier. Main and Preston, Main and Prairie, Main and Texas avenue, Preston and San Jacinto.

District No. 11—Third Ward, J. Snowball, carrier. Dallas and Austin, McKinney and LaBranch, Dallas and Crawford, McKinney and Hamilton, Lamar and Hutchins, Texas avenue and Crawford.

District No. 12—Fifth Ward, H L. Scott, carrier. Montgomery and Harrington, Hardy and Brooks, M. K. & T. Depot, Clark and Sumpter, Chestnut and Waverly.

District No. 13—Fourth Ward, South, J. R. Wilson, carrier. Milam and Rusk, Main and Walker, Capitol and Smith, Main and Rusk

District No. 14—Third Ward, Wm. Giles, carrier. Texas avenue and San Jacinto, Texas avenue and Austin, Prairie and Crawford, Rusk and Crawford Rusk and San Jacinto, Congress and Austin, Crawford and Commerce.

District No. 15—Fourth Ward, North, at Greenough. Preston and Tenth street.

District No 16—T. D. Britt, Carrier Third Ward and Fourth Ward, South Smith and Tuam, Caroline and McGowan.

Observe well the following: Have your mail addressed to street and number, to secure prompt delivery, and in mailing letters use the street boxes as far as possible. If loss or error occur in your mail, report the same to the Postmaster, who will investigate; and, if necessary, refer the matter to the Postoffice Inspector, for further proceedings. If you change your address, report the same promptly to the Superintendent of City Mails, giving your new location explicitly.

RATES OF POSTAGE:

POSTAL CARDS, one cent each, go, without further charge, to all parts of the United States and Canada. Cards of foreign countries (within the Postal Union) two cents each. Postal cards are unmailable with any writing of printing on the address side, except the direction, or with anything pasted upon or attached to them

ALL LETTERS, to all parts of the United States and Canada, two cents for each ounce or fraction thereof.

LOCAL, OR "DROP" LETTERS, that is, for the city or town where deposited, two cents, where the Carrier System is established; and one cent where there is no Carrier System.

FIRST CLASS—Letters and all other written matter, whether sealed or unsealed, and all other matter sealed, nailed, sewed, tied or fastened in any manner, so that it cannot be easily examined, two cents for each ounce, or fraction thereof.

SECOND CLASS—Only for publishers and news agents, one cent per pound Newspapers and periodicals—regular publications—can be mailed by the public at the rate of one cent for each four ounces, or fraction thereof

THIRD CLASS—Printed matter, in unsealed wrappers only—all matter inclosed in notched envelopes must pay letter rates—one cent for each two ounces or fraction thereof, which must be fully prepaid; this includes books, circulars, chromos, engravings, hand-bills, lithographs, music, pamphlets, proof sheets and manuscript accompanying the same, reproductions by the electric pen, hectographs, metalographs, papyographs, and, in short, any reproduction upon paper, by any process, except handwriting and the copying press.

FOURTH CLASS—All mailable matter not included in the three preceding classes, which is so prepared for mailing as to be easily withdrawn from the wrapper and examined, one cent per ounce or fraction thereof. Limit of weight, four pounds; full prepayment compulsory.

RE-FORWARDING—Letters will be forwarded from one postoffice to another, upon written request of the person addressed, without additional charge; but unclaimed packages cannot be returned to the sender, until stamps are furnished to pay the return postage.

PERMISSABLE WRITING—No writing is permitted on Third or Fourth Class matter, except as follows: The name and address of the sender on the outside or inside of the package, preceded by the word "from." On the wrapper may also be written the names and number of articles inclosed. The sender is further allowed to mark a word or passage in a book or paper, to which he desires to call special attention. He may also write a simple inscription or dedication upon the cover or blank leaves of a book or pamphlet. There may be attached to articles of merchandise, by tag or label, a mark, number, name or letter, for the purposes of identification. Printed circulars may contain the written name of the sender, or the address and the date. Any other writing on Third or Fourth Class matter will subject the package to letter rates of postage and render the sender liable to a fine of $10 for each offense. Printed matter may be inclosed with Fourth Class matter, but the whole package is subject to the rate of one cent per ounce or fraction thereof.

MONEY ORDERS.

For Orders for sums not exceeding	$ 2 50	3 cents
Over $ 2 50 and not exceeding	5 00	5 "
" 5 00 " " "	10 00	8 "
" 10 00 " " "	20 00	10 "
" 20 00 " "	30 00	12 "
" 30 00 " " "	40 00	15 "
" 40 00 " " "	50 00	18 "
" 50 00 " " "	60 00	20 "
" 60 00 " " "	75 00	25 "
" 75 00 " " "	100 00	30 "

NOTE—The maximum amount for which a single Money Order may be issued at an office designated as a "Money Order Office," is $100, and at an office designated as a "Limited Money Order Office," $5. When a larger sum is to be sent, additional Orders must be obtained. But Postmasters are instructed to refuse to issue in one day to the same Remitter, and in favor of the same Payee, on any one Postoffice of the Fourth Class, Money Orders amounting in the aggregate to more than $300, as such office might not have funds sufficient for immediate payment of any large amount Fractions of a cent are not to be introduced.

FOREIGN POSTAGE.

The rates for letters are for the half ounce or fraction thereof, and those for newspapers for two ounces or fraction thereof:

To Great Britain and Ireland, France, Spain, all parts of Germany, including Austria, Denmark, Switzerland, Italy, Russia, Norway, Sweden, Turkey European and Asiatic), Egypt, letters five cents; newspapers one cent for each two ounces or fraction thereof.

To Australia, letters via San Francisco (except to New South Wales), five cents; via Brindisi, fifteen cents; newspapers via San Francisco, two cents. via Brindisi, four cents.

China—letters, via San Francisco, five cents, via Brindisi, thirteen cents; four cents for each paper not weighing over four ounces.

British India, Italian mail—letters five cents; newspapers, one cent for two ounces

Japan—letters, via San Francisco, five cents; newspapers, one cent for two ounces.

ADDITIONS

To the City of Houston, Outside of City Limits.

Names.	Direction from Courthouse.	Nearest Street Car Route.
Baker's	N. W.	No. 6.
Brady's	E.	No. 1 and G. LaP. & H. R'y
Brashear's, J	N. W.	Nos. 7 and 8.
Brashear's, S	N. W.	Nos. 7 and 8.
Belle Plain	N.	Nos. 7 and 8.
Brunner	N. W.	No. 8.
Cascara	N. E.	No. 9.
Cage	N. E.	No. 9.
Chew, F. F	N. W.	Nos. 7 and 8.
Empire	S.	No. 2.
Fair Ground	S.	Nos. 2 and 4.
Fair Ground Extension	S.	Nos. 2 and 4.
Fairview	S. W.	No 4.
Houston Heights	N. W.	No. 8.
Kœhler's	N. W.	Nos 7 and 8.
Magnolia	N. W.	Nos. 7 and 8.
Oak Lawn	E.	Galv. LaPorte & Ho R'y.
Oak Lawn Annex	E.	Galv. LaPorte & Ho. R'y.
Riverside Park	N.	Nos. 7 and 8.
Shearn's	N. E.	No. 6.
Turner's	S. W.	No. 2.
Woodland Heights	N. E.	No. 6.
Y. M. R. E. & B. Assn.	E	G. H. & H. R'd.

HARRIS COUNTY TOWNS and R. R. STATIONS.

DIRECTION AND MILES FROM HOUSTON.

*Addickes, 22 miles west of Houston.
Aldine, on I. & G. N. R'd, 19 miles from Houston.
Allen, on G. LaP. & H. R'y, 8 miles from Houston.
Alameda, on I. & G. N. R'd.
Bayland, 30 miles southeast.
*Bayview, (Morgan's Point), 32 miles southeast
Beelers', on Texas Western R'y, 17 miles.
*Cedar Bayou, 35 miles east.
Chaney Junction, on H. & T. C. and G. H. & S. A. R'ys, 1 mile.
*Crosby, on T. & N. O. R'd, 21 miles.
Cross Timbers, on I. & G. N. R'd, 5 miles.
Clinton, on Tex. Trans. Co.'s R'd, 8 miles.
*Cypress, on H. & T. C. R'd, 26 miles.
Cypress Top, on G. H. & H. R'd, 9 miles.
Deep water, on G. LaP. & H. R'y, 12 miles.
Deer Park, on G. LaP. & H. R'y, 15 miles.
*Eureka, on H. & T. C. R'd, 7 miles.
Erin, on G. C. & S. F. R'y, 12 miles.
Fauna, on T. & N. O. R'd, 12 miles.
Genoa, on G. H. & H. R'd, 15 miles.
Green's Bayou, on T. & N. O. R'd, 8 miles.
Gum Island, on H. & T. C. R'd, 13 miles.
Habermacher, on Texas Western R'y, 22 miles.
*Harrisburg, on G. H. & H. R'd and G. LaP. & H. R'y, 5 miles.
Hillendahl, 12 miles west.
*Hockley, on H. & T. C. R'd, 36 miles.
*Humble, on H. E. & W. T. R'y, 17 miles.
Jeannetta, on S. A. & A. P. R'y, 10 miles.

Kleiber, on H. E. & W. T. R'y, 19 miles.
Klein, 22 miles northwest
Koreville, 22 miles northwest.
*LaPorte, on G. LaP. & H. R'y, 22 miles.
Locke, on H. E. & W. T. R'y, 9 miles.
Lords, on H. E. & W. T. R'y, 18 miles.
Lotus, on G. H. & S. A. R'y, 15 miles.
*Lynchburg, on Buffalo Bayou, 22 miles east.
Morgan's Point, on Galveston Bay. 22 miles s. e.
Pasadena, on G. LaP. & H. R'y, 10 miles.
Pearland, on G. C. & S. F. R'y, 14 miles.
Pierce Junction, on I. & G. N. R'd, 10 miles.
Piney Point, on Texas Western R'y, 12 miles.
Prairie, on I. & G. N. R'd, 13 miles.
Rose Hill, 36 miles northwest.
San Jacinto, on Buffalo Bayou, 22 miles east.
Sheldon, on T. & N. O. R'd, 17 miles.
Spring, on I. & G. N. R'd, 23 miles.
*Stella, on G. H. & S. A. R'y, 10 miles.
Steubner, 36 miles northwest.
Tewena, on G. H. & S. A. R'y, 5 miles.
Thayer, on G. LaP. & H. R'y, 16 miles.
Thompsons, on H. & T. C. R'd, 18 miles.
Volmer, 10 miles northwest.
*Websterville, on G. H. & H. R'd, 21 miles.
*Westfield, on I. & G. N. R'd, 19 miles.
Westheimer, on Texas Western R'y, 5 miles.
Zimbi, on Texas Western R'y, 21 miles.

* Postoffice.

CITIZENS' ELECTRIC LIGHT AND POWER CO.

Office, No. 90 Main street. Plant, Race street, east bank Buffalo Bayou. Route No. 9.

HOUSTON GAS LIGHT CO.

Office and Works, 1515 Commerce street. Route No. 11.

HOUSTON WATER WORKS CO.

Office, 316 Fannin street. Works, 23 Artesian Place. Routes Nos. 6, 7 and 8.

LIST OF PRINCIPAL TOWNS IN TEXAS,

—WITH—

Name of Railroad on which Located, Distance in Miles from Houston. Local Railroad Fare, 3c. per Mile.

HOUSTON TO	RAILROAD	MILES
Albany	T. C	375
Alexander	"	284
Allen	H. & T. C	288
Anna	"	308
Aquilla	T. C	209
Austin	H. & T. C	166
Arcola	I. & G. N	21
Alleyton	G., H. & S. A	81
Alvarado	G., C. & S. F	327
Benchly	H. & T. C	108
Brenham	"	72
Bremond	"	143
Bryan		100
Burton	"	85
Boerne	S. A. & A. P	268
Beaumont	T. & N. O	84
Brownwood	G., C. & S. F	342
Belton	"	222
Carbon	T. C	327
Calvert	H. & T. C	129
Carmine	"	92
Chappel Hill	"	62
College	"	95
Corsicana	"	211
Courtney	"	63
Crockett	I. & G. N	113
Cisco	T. C	341
Chenango	I. & G. N	37
Columbia	"	50
Corrigan	H. E. & W. T	93
Cuero	S. A. & A. P	135
Columbus	G., H. & S. A	85
Coleman	G., C. & S. F	374
Cameron	"	184
Cleburne	"	313

LIST OF PRINCIPAL CITIES CONTINUED.

HOUSTON TO	RAILROAD	MILES
Dallas	H. & T. C	265
DeLeon	T. C	306
Dublin	"	293
Denison	H. & T. C	338
Dayton	T. & N. O	36
Elgin	H. & T. C	139
Ennis	"	231
Erath	T. C	353
Eagle Lake	S. A. & A. P	51
Ferris	H. & T. C	246
Faulkner	T. Mid	242
Fowler	T. C	230
Fort Worth	F. W. & N. O.	287
Franklin	I. & G. N	228
Flatonia	G., H. & S. A	122
Garrett	H. & T. C	234
Giddings	"	107
Grapeland	I. & G. N	127
Galveston	I. & G. N	50
	G., C. & S. F	50
Georgetown	I. & G. N	323
Groesbeeck	H. & T. C	170
Gainesville	G., S. & S. F	406
Harrison	W. & N. W	178
Hempstead	H. & T. C	51
Hammond	"	138
Hearne	"	121
Hutchins	"	255
Henderson	I. & G. N	226
Huntsville	"	75
Hico	T. C	271
Howe	H. & T. C	319
Harwood	G., H. & S. A	148
Hallettsville	S. A. & A. P.	100
Honey Grove	G., C. & S. F	447
Iredell	T. C	260

LIST OF PRINCIPAL CITIES CONTINUED.

HOUSTON TO	RAILROAD	MILES
Jacksonville	I. & G. N	178
Kosse	H. & T. C	154
Kauffman	Tex. Mid	262
Kyle	I. & G. N	354
Kerrville	S. A. & A. P	308
LaGrange	M., K. & T	96
Llano	A. & N. W	265
Lovelady	I. & G. N	100
Longview	"	233
Laredo	"	566
Ledbetter	H. & T. C	99
Luling	G., H. & S. A	157
Liberty	T. & N. O	42
Lake Charles	"	145
Livingston	H., E. & W. T	71
Lufkin	"	118
Lampasas	G., C. & S. F	269
Mexia	H. & T. C	181
Millican	"	81
Miller	"	260
McKinney		296
Melissa	"	303
McDade	"	129
Marshal	T. & Pac.	256
Marlin	W. & N. W	160
Morgan	T. C	241
Mineola	I. & G. N	241
Moscow	H., E. & W. T	87
Marion	G., H. & S. A	190
Meridian	G., C. & S. F	276
McGregor	"	239
Milano	"	170
Navasota	H. & T. C	71
New Braunfels	I. & G. N	381
Nacogdoches	H. E. & W. T	138
Overton	I. & G. N	210

LIST OF PRINCIPAL CITIES CONTINUED.

HOUSTON TO	RAILROAD	MILES
Orange	T. & N O	106
Palmer	H. & T. C	239
Plano	"	283
Palestine	I. & G. N	151
Perry	W. & N. W	168
Paige	H. & T. C	118
Plantersville	G., C. & S. F	181
Paris	"	465
Richland	H. & T. C	199
Rice	"	221
Richardson	"	277
Reagan	W. & N. W	152
Ross	T. C	197
Roberts	Tex. Mid	286
Rockdale	I. & G. N	271
Round Rock	"	313
Richmond	G., H. & S. A	33
Sherman	H. & T. C	329
San Marcos	I. & G. N	363
Scurry	Tex. Mid	254
Sour Lake	T. & N. O	64
Schulenburg	G., H. & S. A	110
Seguin	"	178
San Antonio	"	216
San Angelo	G., C. & S. F	440
Sealy	Texas Western	51
Thornton	H. & T. C	162
Trinity	I. & G. N	86
Troupe	"	196
Texarkana	"	330
Tyler		216
Taylor	"	296
Terrell	Tex. Mid	273
Wellborn	H. & T. C	89
Wootan	"	139
Wortham	"	189

LIST OF PRINCIPAL CITIES CONTINUED.

HOUSTON TO	RAILROAD	MILES
Willis	I. & G. N	47
Waco	W. & N. W	186
Whitney	T. C	219
Walnut Springs	"	250
Waxahachie	C. T. & N. W	246
Wallis	S. A. & A. P	44
Weimar	G., H. & S. A	100
Waelder	"	135
Weatherford	G., C. & S. F	352
Yoakum	S. A. & A. P	117

Houston Com'l College

Book-keeping, Shorthand, Typewriting

—AND—

Higher Preparatory Courses

TAUGHT BY EXPERIENCED TEACHERS.

Call on, or address

HOUSTON COMMERCIAL COLLEGE,

HOUSTON, TEXAS.

ALBANY DENTISTS,

610 MAIN STREET.

FULL UPPER OR LOWER SET BEST TEETH, $7.00.

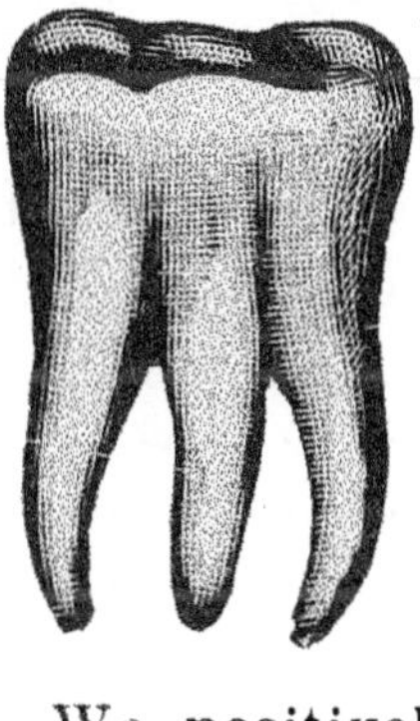

No Better Made,
No matter how much you pay.

We extract teeth free when new teeth are made.

Gold Fillings...........	$1.50 up.
Platinum...	1 00
Silver and Amalgam ...	.75
Extracting Teeth........	.25

We positively *Extract Teeth Without Pain.* Four Operators. We have the entire floor of Heiner Block.

T. F. BOYD, H. J. RAMACKER,
G. R. WITTENBERG, H. HAMMOND.

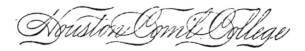

NUMERICAL LIST OF CONTENTS.

Lightning Source UK Ltd.
Milton Keynes UK
UKHW022116081218
333475UK00006B/176/P

9 780483 173125